FIXING AMERICAN
ELEMENTARY EDUCATION

FIXING AMERICAN ELEMENTARY EDUCATION

A Parent's Guide

Patrick M. Dallabetta

Library of Congress Control Number: 2024910052

ISBN: 979-8-89228-166-9   (Paperback)
ISBN: 979-8-89228-167-6   (eBook)

Printed in the United States of America

CONTENTS

Fixing American Elementary Education
A Parent's Guide

INTRODUCTION

Author's Note: Important recommendations and points are highlighted throughout this book.

If you want your children to succeed in school, you need to get involved! You should understand the school program your children are to receive and, if not satisfactory, you need to be active in making changes or even provide help with instruction at home!

The performance of American school students, at all educational levels, has continued to plummet for many years. American students do not perform as well as some countries described as third world. **"Fixing American Elementary Schools: A Parents' Guide" was written to help parents understand what they can do to improve elementary education for their children.** I continue to hear comments like "My child can't read or spell" or "My child can't write." A very sad comment came from one parent who said "My child was an A student all through public elementary school and his teachers loved him, but now he is enrolled in an excellent parochial high school and failing. What is wrong and how can this happen?" This book will attempt to answer these questions.

I am going to show you what to look for when your child starts or returns to school. If you want your children to be successful, you should expect quality instruction. Following the recommendations in this book will provide you with information that may mean the difference between success and failure for your child.

This book is meant to be a learning tool for parents. If you care about your child receiving a quality elementary education, you need to understand what makes a school good. **"Fixing American Elementary Schools: A Parents' Guide" will give you the knowledge you need to make sure your child receives the best possible elementary education.** Parents need to get involved and active in their child's elementary school program. Reading this book will help you with that process.

Your child's elementary years build a foundation for success in later school experiences. Instruction in the first years of elementary school must be effective. Children need to learn how to read and write with competence. They need to be able to write legibly, starting with printing letters and eventually using script. They need a solid foundation in mathematics. Science is critical and the movement to combine science with technology and engineering concepts in STEM Programs (Science, Technology, Engineering, and Math Education) is especially effective because of its hands-on problem-based learning. American students are sadly geographically illiterate, so how can we expect them to understand the international challenges and issues we face in the world today? Students need to understand the history of our country and how our government works. They need a solid understanding of our Constitution and Bill of Rights. These subjects should be the main emphasis of elementary education, especially in the upper elementary grades.

In writing **"Fixing American Elementary Schools: A Parent's Guide"**, I decided to make it less of a professional publication by avoiding extensive references that support the principles I discuss. **But the information in this book is supported by an immense amount of effective educational research in other words, what works best in schools.** Everything in this book is based on methods that are essential for quality teaching. This book is intended for parents and not a learning tool for teachers, even though they would benefit from the information in the book.

Most importantly, this book is not an indictment on all of America's teachers. Most teachers love children and truly care about their growth as students. Although some are better than others, even some of our best teachers must work within a system they often have no control, far too often an ineffective instructional program.

Whether it is their teacher education programs and out of touch college professors, the opinions and practices of other teachers, or uninformed administrators, the results generally aren't often as good as they could be.

Too many teachers don't understand what instructional methods work best, so parents need to understand what is important. Most teachers rely on the preparation they receive in college. Some teacher training programs are better than others and I have learned that you can't depend on administrators, or even some college instructors, to fully understand the concepts they need to create the most effective instruction. They may be products of instructors who do not teach methods that are effective and instead, teach how or what they believe is good or what they may have used as teachers themselves.

Worse yet, new teachers are normally required to use instructional programs required by the administration of the school that may not be effective. They may not be using what instructional programs that work best. **I can assure you that most teachers, while dedicated and love children, may not fully understand all the strategies needed to create the best outcomes.** Most of the new teachers I have dealt with in my career are dedicated and hard-working people that want to succeed. Unfortunately, this may be difficult if they are not using effective teaching methods and programs. Loving children and being a hard worker is great, but not enough.

There is a significant difference in the quality of various college teacher education programs. This is especially true of many liberal colleges that have traditionally been considered the most prestigious colleges in America. This became painfully clear during extensive national teacher recruitments during my career.

I discovered that some of the most well-prepared teachers enter the education field with advanced degrees. Their colleges require all future teachers to declare a major for their undergraduate program. For example, a college student would decide to be a mathematics or biology major and spend the first four years of their college education studying that field of expertise. After graduating, they are required to spend their entire graduate program studying education, which includes extensive student teaching experiences. As a result, those teachers become more effective in the classroom because they are more knowledgeable in their field of expertise. They spend their entire graduate program in education learning how to teach effectively.

The problem with some college programs is that they don't always focus on effective instructional strategies and important curricular efforts. Teachers often get excited about new ideas, originating from college professors that have created some new oddball method of teaching. Such was the case with the teachers and professors still pushing programs like whole language, which put emphasis on memorizing words in reading without teaching the code of the phonetic English language.

If you want more information, **I suggest you purchase a more comprehensive view of the subject discussed in "American Elementary Education: The Longest Pandemic" that is available online or on my website patrickdallabetta.com.** It provides comprehensive information to help parents evaluate and clearly understand the education their children receive. I have also purposely highlighted some of the text in this book to support many recommendations.

Lastly, you will notice that I have not organized the information in this book with chapters. Rather, I have chosen to use recommendations that you should consider as a parent.

RECOMMENDATION 1
Get Involved in Your Child's School

Get active and involved in understanding what is happening in your elementary school and district. Don't wait to meet with the school staff until after school has started. Make it a priority to meet your children's teachers before the first day of school.

Parents are the most important factor in making sure children receive the best possible instruction. Most elementary schools schedule a parent night where the administration and teachers discuss and explain programming. They may talk about important issues such as student discipline and instructional programs. At these meetings the parents may even meet their children's teachers who discuss their expectations and instructional programs. Parent meetings are often scheduled after the first few weeks of school. If no parent meetings are scheduled, I would be very concerned.

Ask to meet with your child's teacher before school starts. I would not be comfortable if school personnel are unwilling to meet with you before school begins. **The most effective schools schedule parent meetings to help parents understand their programs and expectations as soon as possible.** The meetings provide valuable information that assists parents in understanding what instruction their child is to receive. **It would be best if parent meetings are scheduled before the start or at least the first week of school. If you are not satisfied with the information you receive after school has started, you are already at a disadvantage! But at least you have the time to make necessary changes.**

One of the best elementary school programs I have seen in my career required teachers to make a home visit to every student enrolled in their classroom prior to the first day of school. This gave the teachers the opportunity to meet their students, provide parents details on what their children are to learn, discuss student discipline and management programs, and answer questions. Teachers met their students and gave them extensive information about the performance outcomes they expect at the end of the school year. A direct contact with parents is especially important in the first few elementary grades.

I encourage you to be active in choosing the best teachers for your children. Normally creating classroom lists is completely up to school personnel. However, you need to get involved in the process because you want the best for your children. **Although you should be careful as a parent about what you hear from other parents, they may give you good information about teachers, especially if the information is consistent among parents. I suggest you check the previous student performance by teachers on state testing programs, often available at your state department of education website. Request teachers whose students consistently perform at higher levels.**

You have the right to request specific teachers but expect that your request may not be approved. **Put your teacher requests in writing and you should expect a response before school starts.** There are many factors used by school personnel to develop class lists. They normally try to create even classes of boys and girls and consider the level of performance of the returning children. They may consider children having questionable behavior so as not to load up any class with too many potential discipline problems. This can be an issue when a particular teacher is assigned more of these children because the teacher is considered a stronger disciplinarian.

There are many current issues that have created more interest in what is happening in schools. These include critical race theory, gender dysphoria and identification, school safety, and curriculum issues to name a few. **If you want your child to get the best education possible, you need to understand the school policies that address these issues to your satisfaction.** Simple answers are needed such as will my daughter be forced to use a bathroom with a biological boy who might consider himself a girl? Will my child be taught reading with a phonics program? Many educational institutions have gone too far and some policies are just nuts!

Board Meetings and Call to the Public

Most districts allow comments from the public during the "call to the public" on most school board agendas. Attending school board meetings can be very informational, especially when you have an issue you feel important. It is appropriate to address issues at lower levels beginning with the teacher and, if necessary, the principal at your child's school. If the answers you receive aren't satisfactory, don't hesitate to take your questions to the next level. This may mean a meeting with the superintendent or even the school district governing board.

If you need to attend a school board meeting and wish to make a comment, you may be required to sign a request form to speak prior to the meeting and your input may be limited by time requirements. Your input should be included when school board minutes are created. If your input is not referenced in subsequent school board meeting minutes, something isn't right! You can present your request to speak at the meeting to the administration prior to the scheduled meeting. You should specifically request your input be included at the next formal school board meeting. **Most issues can be resolved with the teachers or administration at the school, but don't be afraid to attend school board meetings and make yourself heard!**

School board members are generally not allowed to respond to your questions or concerns at board meetings during a call to the public. Do not expect board member to comment on your concerns or questions in the meeting. However, make it clear that you want a response to your questions or comments at some point after the meeting. You have a right to speak and voice your opinion, especially when you do so in an appropriate manner and observe proper decorum. It might even be helpful to read your information and then give your written input in writing to whomever is keeping the notes for the meeting. Make sure your input is added to agenda minutes after the meeting. You may be asked to limit your input, but I think limiting input to just a couple of minutes may border on the side of illegal. But it is important that you not try to dominate the entire meeting. Make your point clear and then listen to what other issues are discussed at the meeting.

You may request your issue be placed on a future school board meeting agenda. If not requested at a board meeting during the call to the public, you should do so in writing in a timely fashion, perhaps even two weeks before the meeting is scheduled. Normally agendas must be publicly posted at least 24 hours before meetings. I tried very hard to post my agenda several days before my meetings. A good agenda takes time as superintendents must provide backup materials in support of proposed recommendations. My board meeting agendas always included my recommendations in writing. When I presented an issue without a recommendation, I always included the statement "action as deemed appropriate by the governing board." If the administration refuses to add your agenda item, I suggest you ask them to put their decision not to do so in writing. I would then request to speak at the meeting during the call to the public. If there is no call to the public during a school board meeting, I would formally again request you be added to the agenda at a future meeting. Also note that "special" board meetings may not allow a call to the public or parental input. Try to limit your input to regularly scheduled meetings. Review posted agendas so that you know when an important item is to be addressed.

Always create some type of formal documentation of your interactions and comments or concerns. It is important to have a record of your input and it is important to make sure your written record has specific information. Include dates, times, who was involved in the discussion, as well as your input as a parent or district constituent. Accurate information is essential, so spare no details.

Most importantly, make sure you elect school board members more sympathetic to parent and student issues. Sadly, some parents have recently been labeled "domestic terrorists". Believe me, if you abide by reasonable protocols, don't worry about being labeled a troubled parent. Don't be afraid to push for beliefs you feel important in schools. That is the only way you can expect positive changes in American elementary schools!

It would be helpful to attend a parent-teacher organization meetings to meet other parents. These organizations are meant to support their schools and teachers. But you can get important information that might impact your children. Often problems are discussed that are important and it always helps to know the perspectives of other parents. If you have concerns, you may want to share them with other parents who might have their own opinions which may also be important.

Parents can be the most important check on quality instruction. For example, the reading program at your school may not include phonics. A good phonics program is incredibly important, and you may have no choice as a parent to change or select another school if phonics reading programs are not used. In some cases, you may need to make sure you provide that instruction at home. There are literally dozens of excellent programs in all curricular areas that will help parents supplement instruction. Some of the phonics programs are available in a computer-based format. Well prepared elementary students come from homes that are active in helping children learn so never forget how important you are as parents!

RECOMMENDATION 2
Find Information That Helps You Evaluate the Quality of Your Elementary School

Parents can find valuable information about school programs with the touch of a computer key. You should know how successful your school is by examining its performance.

Parents can easily find information about the quality of elementary schools. It is important that parents understand how their schools perform in comparison to other schools in the area and state. In this case, the internet is your friend and the easiest way to evaluate the performance of the school serving your children. In fact, you can check the performance of every school in the state and nation. **Some of the following websites are very helpful in providing important information about schools.**

1. State Department of Education Websites
2. School District Websites (Remember that school websites are designed to market the school so be careful with the information.)
3. https://schooldigger.com
4. https://niche.com
5. https://nces.ed.gov
6. https://greatschools.org
7. https://usnews.org
8. https://publiccharters.com
9. https://fraserinstitute *(for Canadians)*

Examine the ranking or rating of your school by accessing public information on your state's department of education. For example, one state assigns grades to schools based on a myriad of factors, the most important of which is student growth and performance.

Why would you want to put your child in a school that is rated as a "C" or "D" school?

There is a massive amount of information on these sites. Parents can check and compare performance of all schools in their state and examine other factors that influence the performance of schools. Demographic information, numbers of English language learners, achievement and performance, school ratings, philosophy, and schedules are available to name a few. You can also find out how many teachers at a school meet all certification requirements and how many children are meeting performance requirements.

When you access one of the above websites mentioned above, look for the following:

1. **School rank information** (ranks the school in comparison to all other schools in the district and state.)
2. **Rating of the school** from the website or from the state's education department.
3. **Performance information** (percentages of children meeting required standards).
4. **Demographic** information.
5. **Teacher information**.
6. **Percentage of English language learners (an increasingly important factor.)** High numbers of non-English speaking children may not be bad. However, it does mean that teachers must place more emphasis on teaching students basic English. There is some good in exposing your children to a second language. My worry is that spending so much time with children that have no command of English may put important instruction for English dominant children at risk for other important skills.

You can also access information about charter schools in your area on the internet. Charter schools offer some programs not available in public schools and may be a good alternative. **As of the publication of this book, charter schools are generally producing slightly better student achievement than public schools.**

Achievement Test Scores

Most states require annual testing of public and charter school children and the results of the test scores are normally made available to parents. **You need to make sure you review the results of the achievement test scores of your children.** There is great value in knowing how your children are progressing in school as compared to other children in the school, state, and nation. Although testing requirements may differ from state to state, you should examine the information, giving you a better understanding of the performance in the basic subjects of reading, language arts, and mathematics. Some states have added science or other subjects that are tested. Make sure you understand the performance of your children in those subjects. It is important to realize that a good command of the English language will help you be successful in other subjects, including science education.

The performance of your children will help you better understand areas that your children excel or need help. Most educators are required to concentrate on children that are not performing and might need help. It is possible your children score higher as compared to other students and they may qualify for additional assistance as a highly performing child. The funding for talented and gifted children and programs for children achieving at very high levels is poor even though most gifted programs may come under the umbrella of special education programing. I was the superintendent of a large school district that spent millions of dollars on special education programs but only had a budget of $5,000 for gifted children, something I quickly addressed. All schools should do a better job of serving high achievers!

There is a difference between a gifted child and a child who is motivated and works hard to achieve at high levels. I personally believe we do very little to meet the needs of both high achieving and gifted children because school districts devote most of funding resources to serve children who are not performing well or have an identified disability. Schools should be providing more accelerated programs for both gifted and high achieving students. Unfortunately, American education does a much better job of trying to meet the needs of students who are not performing well, often at the expense of higher achieving students.

The point is you as a parent should better understand how your children are doing in school as compared to other students. Then you need to become your child's most important advocate. Push for help when needed and make sure the school allows children to move ahead as they master the skills appropriate to their instructional level. Meet with the teachers and work to make sure the teachers understand the importance of meeting the individual needs of your children.

I remember meeting with the mother of one of my children's best friends who told me she loved our school but felt her daughter was a little bored with the program. As parents we like to think our children are the "best", but I carefully listened to her concerns. I reviewed the student's performance on the state mandated testing program which indicated very high performance and authorized a full testing of the student by the school psychologist. After administering an intelligence test, we determined she was a truly gifted child. The parent had legitimate concerns and we quickly moved to implement measures to better meet her instructional needs. **The fact that parents can initiate these measures will be discussed in a section of this book that deals with special education.**

RECOMMENDATION 3
School Choice and Vouchers

Explore all possibilities when choosing a school. If you are unhappy with a school, there are likely options for inter-district transfers of students or enrollment in a charter schoos. This recommendation examines the positive benefits for parents as they analyze educational alternatives.

Having some choices in American education is positive and will ultimately push all schools to improve. The lack of satisfactory student and school performance resulted in the establishment of the charter school movement. As parents, you may choose what schools your children attend whether public, charter, or perhaps even parochial schools. Most parochial schools result in an additional monetary commitment that may not be possible for many parents. But there is a serious effort to allow vouchers to be spent for parochial school enrollment. This may not happen where you live, but the effort is ongoing.

Generally, charter schools are performing better than public schools because I believe they may have more flexibility in programing. As a former public educator, I find that very sad. But it is clear to me that some American school programs have not sufficiently improved over the years. Parents have begun to understand the need for better education for children and actively explore alternatives. Many parents and educators have begun to understand the shortcomings of public schools, resulting in the charter school movement. That is also the reason I think public schools will continue to improve. **Had the instruction at public schools been good enough there would have never been a need for charter schools.** There are some elementary school programs that are so good parents need to stand in line to enroll their children.

This makes it more important to understand what is effective if choices are limited to public and charter schools. There are some very effective public schools in our country, but far too many schools are not as productive as they should be. There are almost 8,000 charter schools in the United States and the charter school movement is exploding. Parents may be able to choose among the almost 100,000 public elementary schools in our country. But there are almost 24,000 private schools that might be more appropriate for your child. Take the time to evaluate schools to ensure your children receive the best possible education. Giving your children a good education is one of the most important parental gifts.

Use the Internet to help you look for school enrollment options. There are several websites that can provide important performance information. Consider looking for schools that consistently rank high. Often ranking information is provided for all the schools in your state. **I even suggest you consider schools that carry labels such as "basic', "traditional", "fundamental" or "academy"**. These schools usually offer systematic phonics in their instructional programs and often achieve better performance than other schools. They also may provide more accelerated learning opportunities. Look at their performance as compared to other public and charter schools in your area.

During one of my wife's stay in the hospital for a week, her nurse, knowing I was a former school superintendent, told me she and her husband were worried about what school to send their new kindergarten student. I told her that there was a simple solution to her concern. **Using my portable computer, I searched the available schools close to their residence and found a "traditional" public school close enough to their home. The performance at that school was the best in the district where they reside.** In looking at their instructional program, I discovered the school was using the Spalding Writing Road to Reading Program, an intensive phonics reading and writing program. After showing her how I arrived at that recommendation she told me "You should write a book for parents on how to choose a school." That comment was somewhat ironic!

RECOMMENDATION 4
Make Sure Your Schools Place Emphasis on Student Safety

In view of the terrible incidents of extreme violence in recent years, school safety is one of the most critical factors for all schools. You need to be comfortable that your school has done everything possible to protect your children.

Most school districts are taking safety issues very seriously and that is a good thing. I am certainly not an expert on school safety, but I have seen enough school safety issues in my career to suggest consideration of the following ideas.

1. **Every school should have only one entrance and one exit, and it should always be carefully monitored. All other entrance or exit points should always be locked.**
2. **A list of people authorized to take children out of school or transport children should be maintained.**
3. **Every school should have tall fences that provide difficult entry.** A short chain link fence is not good enough. All schools should provide fences that maintain the best possible security. There is a good reason for fences and walls.
4. **I am an enthusiastic proponent of school resource police officers (SROs) for every school in our country.** If used effectively, they are an excellent resource. They work and interact with students, teachers, and parents. They can provide a better level of security and assist with disciplinary issues, which is one of the biggest instructional time wasters in our schools. SROs should help monitor entry and exit points and provide more immediate response to any security problem. They can also be used to augment instruction or work with extracurricular activities. I have been involved in some very

dangerous and difficult situations as an administrator. Not having immediate help proved very frustrating.

5. **Every school should have video cameras to monitor entrance and exits**. In addition, halls should have cameras. While controversial, I think every classroom should be equipped with a video camera. This recommendation would likely be opposed by many teachers for the simple reason many are not comfortable being monitored as they teach. However, cameras can be a valuable tool to record issues. I was a very lucky beginning teacher. I had an assistant principal who visited my classroom at least once every other week. I never knew when he would visit my class which motivated me to always prepare the best possible lessons. **Some districts have installed video cameras on school buses, so why not classrooms?**

6. **Every school should have an effective night alarm and video surveillance system.** The equipment I have discussed is reasonable in terms of cost and every school should take advantage of technology for safety reasons. Motion detection lights can also help.

7. **Emergency procedures should be practiced often** so that there is no doubt what teachers and their students are supposed to do in every kind of situation.

8. **The use of uniforms is an option and lets everyone know which children belong at the school.**

9. **Law enforcement should be partners in helping to develop emergency plans to handle all varieties of problems.** They are an important resource that schools should regularly use to prepare for the worst possible situation.

Now for a very controversial idea. **This is just a thought and not a recommendation.** Things have gotten so bad I am beginning to think about the possibility of allowing specific school employees to carry a concealed weapon for defense purposes to assist in dealing with emergency situations. Consider the physical layout of the school. In the absence of a SRO, I would also suggest the following:

a. **Designated concealed carriers of weapons should receive intense special training** in the use of firearms, including critical ballistic information. Training could be provided by law enforcement specialists and specific weapons should be consistent among those authorized to carry the weapon.

b. **Carriers of weapons should be carefully screened and trained in procedures necessary to protect the children.** Those designated to carry should undergo intense psychological vetting. They should not be afraid to fire a weapon to protect the children and provided with special insurance to protect them from potential litigation. They should practice regularly with the assistance of law enforcement personnel.

c. **Concealed weapon carriers should be placed strategically according to the physical layout of the school.** Law enforcement should be made aware of the identity of all concealed carriers. Not all teachers should be allowed to carry concealed weapons.

d. **Parents should be aware of all safety procedures** except specific information with regards to strategically placed concealed carriers of deadly force weapons. Authorized carriers should remain anonymous.

e. **Most importantly, schools should regularly interact with law enforcement and regularly update procedures.**

f. **Students and parents should be encouraged to report suspicious behavior from other classmates.** This may be the most important component in the prevention of school violence.

This idea may be too much to think about at this time, especially considering the movement to disarm American citizens. However, based on the number of school shootings, the issue may be worthy of further discussion.

RECOMMENDATION 5
Reading Instruction in Elementary Schools

Ensure your children are being taught reading skills using a phonics program that also includes a penmanship and writing program.

This is especially important in beginning reading programs in elementary school. English is a phonetic language, and it makes no sense to teach our children without understanding the phonetic code of the language.

There are at least 70 phonograms or sounds in English and some of which consist of multiple letters. For example, the sound of OU has four different sounds. For example, the four sounds of OU as in round, OU as in soul, OU as in you, and OU as in country. Children can understand when to use the correct sound for OU if they are taught properly. **It is a proven fact that schools using phonics instruction are more successful in producing competent readers**.

Don't be fooled by teachers who tell you they use phonics in their instructional programs. They may give some attention to the sounds of basic letters but fail to provide essential instruction in the phonic sounds of all letters and combinations of letters, many of which have different sounds and rules. **All children should have a basic understanding of our language by the third grade. New non-English-speaking students should be prioritized and provided extensive assistance with English until they have a better command of the language. That should remain the main emphasis of an educational system.**

Ask what type of phonics program is being used and use the Internet to research that program to be certain your children are receiving appropriate reading instruction. If a teacher mentions "whole language" in their programs be even more concerned. Whole language enthusiasts believe children learn to read naturally if exposed to books. They believe it is better to devote time to ideas and stories rather than teaching children to understand the sounds of letters or combinations of letter sounds. **Teaching children to memorize many whole words is something that may have a negative effect on reading comprehension.**

Many elementary teachers use worksheets that have context clues like pictures in reading instruction worksheets. Then they ask children to identify the correct words that identify the picture. This type of approach can be harmful as children progress, particularly in early grades. **Memorizing most whole words defies logic in helping children learn to sound out the words and probably hurts their understanding of the meaning of words. Children should be taught the rules that are phonics-based. Most of those rules are useful to children in helping pronounce new words. A good phonics program will help children become better spellers.**

Lack of Penmanship Skills

I would like to discuss one of the biggest problems parents may encounter in many elementary schools. **Not only is there a lack of proper phonics instruction, but children should be writing the letters and sounds as they are recited. Penmanship is the third important component of reading instruction which includes auditory, visual, and kinesthetic elements (hearing, seeing, and touching). Writing the words as you sound them out is important. Many American schools have almost totally abandoned or at least diluted penmanship and that is just plain wrong!** I am the proud grandfather of six wonderful children, some of which have poor penmanship skills. I am lucky because they are all very good students regardless of poor instruction early in their education. My youngest grandchild is in middle school and has a difficult time reading the script notes I send him. His primary teachers did not place any emphasis on phonics and penmanship skills. He would not have as many issues to now deal with in his education. Thankfully, he is a wonderful child and will certainly be successful because he wants to achieve and do well in school.

If your schools don't teach phonics and penmanship, you need to teach your children yourself, especially in the absence of other school options. While there are a lot of good resources, one excellent option would be to order phonogram cards from Spalding Education International. They can be contacted through their website **www. spalding.org.** You can purchase their phonogram cards which could be the best thing you could do for your children. Use them regularly with your children and it will help your children read and write more efficiently. The cards should be used daily and will be a tremendous help for children. **I would also recommend parents help children learn and practice penmanship skills using primary penmanship paper.** There are many resources available on the Internet that can be used with children. The time you spend with your children will pay many rewards!

There is one more recommendation that is important for reading instruction. Language arts and reading instruction should dominate a good teacher's time in the first three grades. In fact, I believe **at least 60% of instruction time should be devoted to reading and writing instruction in the primary grades (kindergarten through third grade.)**

If your student is not receiving this type of reading and writing instruction, you need to contact the school and request the program be added or, as a last resort, provide that instruction at home. There are numerous excellent phonics programs available that parents can use to help prepare their children for success. A simple Internet search will give you many examples, some of which are inexpensive and often used by homeschool parents. Many of the programs are computer-based and easy to use. **Don't forget to inform the school of your disappointment if they are not using phonics instruction.**

I have included a short list of some phonics programs you can use with your children if the school does not use intensive phonics instruction in their reading program and you have no other school option. The list contains only some suggestions and not recommendations. It would be helpful if parents chose a program that best fits their needs and schedules. **There are many phonics programs available on the market**

and this list does not contain all the possible choices that may be very effective. I recommend you explore all the options available online. There are several internet sources that can help you decide what to use with your children.

A few other programs you may want to consider:

> Phonic Books Ltd.
> ABCmouse.com
> Teaching Your Child to Read
> Teach Your Child to Read in 100 Easy Lessons
> Reading Eggs
> Hooked on Phonics
> ABC See, Hear, Do Series
> Alpha-Phonics (Storehouse Press)
> Alpha-Phonics (Paradigm)
> All About Reading Learning Press, Inc.
> ABC English Phonics
> Sadlier Phonics

Children educated with positive phonics programs become better readers and spellers, period!

RECOMMENDATION 6
Mathematics Instruction

Help your children with basic mathematics facts. Play math games at home and help them practice basic facts and understand how to address math problems.

Besides reading instruction, mathematics instruction is another of the basic subjects that should be emphasized in school. In my opinion, another **20% of elementary teacher time should be devoted to basic math instruction.** Effective math instruction should involve the development of student's math conceptual understanding, reasoning, and problem-solving skills. Instruction should help children understand patterns, measurement, and a solid understanding of the numeric system. Teachers should teach math in a way that makes sense. They should show students how to solve problems and should use more than one strategy. Then they should understand the differences in the strategies and how each works.

But here is where parents can help. Make it a consistent practice to help your children learn the addition and multiplication facts when they are young. There are also many games you can use to help your children. Check the internet for games that might be fun for your children. Most of the marketed math games are inexpensive and can be very effective in helping children as young as three begin the process of learning important math concepts. Beginning early with your children will reap great rewards when they enter school.

The use of physical materials or models help young children learn math concepts. Students should be allowed to discuss math facts and problems. They should be able to work together to solve problems. I clearly remember math competitions in elementary school where students were given room at blackboards to solve problems, then explain how they arrived at the answer to math computations.

Parents can help by practicing basic math facts at home. I know one family that often uses math fact games at the dinner table. Their children are far ahead of the other children because of the practice they receive at home.

Some math program that parents can purchase, to name a few, are also inexpensive and available on the internet.

Family Math Night
Math Games for Parent Night
Games for Young Minds
Adapted Mind
Happy Numbers
Mathnasium
Math Game Time

RECOMMENDATION 7
Physical and Cultural Geography

Your children should be taught some cultural and physical geography, especially in the upper elementary school grades.

Let's face it, our children are geographic illiterate. It is hard to understand many of the world's problems without a basic knowledge of geography. According to one and most pertinent of the oldest books I have, physical geography considers the globe as a unit in all its features and discusses the mutual relationship of its parts. Geography provides students with a well-rounded perspective, whether it is climate change or the physical consequences of those actions. How many students understand the importance of the actions to disrupt international travel through the Red Sea? Why is the Crimea peninsula important to Russia?

Geography plays an important role in developing children's awareness of relationships between people and the environment. Geography examines the interaction and analyzes the spatial characteristics of all manner of cultural, economic, political, and physical relationships.

Physical geography is also important if the students are to understand the physical world, which would help them understand physical phenomena such as earthquakes, volcanic activity, weather, or other issues such as climate change.

Geography can be very interesting for students. At one school I had students participate in the geography championships. One of the students qualified for the United States Geography Championship, a significant accomplishment. It also provided positive public relations for the school.

Geography instruction should be added to elementary education programs after third grade when children have a command of the English language and mathematics.

RECOMMENDATION 8
Special Education (Things Parents Should Know)

Parents need to clearly understand the special education process if your child has been referred as potentially having some type of disability or learning problem.

Federal and state laws clearly state that all children have access to a free appropriate education. That would include children with disabilities. **It is important parents understand the process used for special education programs.** The main purpose of this information is to assure parents who have children with a disability are not prevented from having a successful school experience. The law provides protections for parents. Some include the following:

1. **Parent involvement is required in the process and protected by law.**
2. **Schools must provide assistive technology or special equipment** that may include computers, equipment, auditory or vision devices, etc.
3. **Children as young as 3 are required to receive special education services if they have an identified disability.** Students with identified serious disabilities may be eligible for service until their 22nd birthday.
4. **Services are required for the following children:**

Specific learning disabilities,
Intellectual disabilities,
Hearing impairments,
Visual impairments,
Emotional disturbance,
Orthopedic impairments,
Autism,

Traumatic brain injuries,
Some health impairments,
Related services such as physical or occupational services,
counseling, speech and language deficits, etc.

People involved in the process may include natural parents, adoptive parents, legal guardians, or individuals acting in place of the natural parents such as grandparents in meetings that discuss the potential performance needs of your children.

I have seen an increasing number of special education services for children diagnosed and assigned a label of "reading dyslexia". Dyslexia is a learning disability that makes reading and language-related tasks harder. More important, parents should know that this includes phonological or auditory problems. It also includes students who find it difficult to rapidly name a letter. Now do you get the picture about the importance of phonics in early reading instruction? **It is my opinion that a lack of intensive phonics instruction in early reading programs is a major factor often resulting in children be given reading dyslexia labels.**

I recommend parents whose children's testing involves reading issues should insist on a more complete phonics program, especially in the early phases of reading instruction. Children with this disorder have trouble reading fluently and often make mistakes even when reading slowly. They may also have poor concentration or forget words easily.

There are many red flags for children with reading dyslexia and are traditionally poor spellers and have trouble with beginning and ending sounds.

Parents should clearly understand the special education process.

1. Identify children that may qualify for special education services. Normally a referral comes from the teacher, but parents have the right to request assistance if they feel their children are struggling. I encourage parents to do so as this is the first step in the special education process. Initial referrals are usually made by the classroom teacher. My youngest child was referred for

services by a teacher who felt she might need some help from a speech and language pathologist. I allowed her to be tested and she really didn't need any significant amount of help. She was just a quiet little girl who is now one of our country's premier forensic chemists who lectures and trains law enforcement personnel all over the country. The main point is parents should be concerned about the seriousness of giving children any disability label.

2. **Testing may be recommended as the second step in the process.** Your child should be evaluated by a certified professional. **Permission to test always requires parent permission.** I recommend that parents allow the testing because it should assist in determining the extent of any possible problem. The purpose of the evaluation is to determine the issue which could be reading, math, or other problems. **Parents must agree in writing to have their children evaluated.** Most often this is the school psychologist or other professionals such as a speech and language specialist. **Parents have the right to request an independent educational evaluation (IEE) paid for by the district. This is especially important if parents do not agree with or have concerns about any recommendation or evaluation.**

3. **Determine eligibility for special education services.** This meeting must always include parents who may challenge the eligibility decision for services.

4. **If the child is eligible for services, a meeting must be scheduled within 30 days of the evaluation. This is an important meeting where the team decides the services needed by creating an individual educational plan (IEP).** This is the meeting where parents may request specific goals for instruction. If your child has been diagnosed with reading dyslexia, you should force the use of phonics in the individual educational plan (IEP). You must be notified of the meeting and may invite people to the meeting who have knowledge or special expertise about your child. **Your signature is required and, if you don't agree with**

the recommendations of the team, can request a due process meeting. You have a right to a copy of the IEP which you need to require specific goals and timelines. The meeting to review progress in meeting goals is required every school year. That is just one of the reasons why parent participation is so important. **If you don't agree with the program, don't sign the IEP!**

5. **Your child must be reevaluated at least every three years, but I strongly suggest you insist on annual for meetings if progress in meeting the instructional goals have not been met. It is important to meet often or at least every year to review measurable progress!**

6. **Parents have the right to ask for help in the process, especially if they disagree or don't understand recommendations.** The Department of Education is often able to provide an advocate which may be important, particularly if there is some disagreement between the school and parents. Advocates should be knowledgeable in the special education process and understand the rules and regulations. Most advocates can be found by contacting your local Department of Education. It is also possible to include other professionals that may be able to help.

It is important to realize the state and federal regulations stress the importance of timelines for the process and input from parents. Special education programs are regularly audited to make sure all deadlines are met. If timelines are not met or parents have not had appropriate input, the school and district may receive an audit citation. Repeated citations may risk federal funding for special education services in a school district. Federal money targeted for special education programs helps, but normally doesn't come close to covering the actual costs of programs. But funding for special programs is important and districts do not want to jeopardize funding for special education programs. **Do not be afraid to insist on specific phonics instruction, particularly in the case of reading disabilities.**

RECOMMENDATION 9

School Disciplinary Programs Should Be Consistent for Schools and Reviewed by Parents

Parents should understand the school's discipline and management program and add their input where appropriate.

Having to deal with disciplinary issues is harmful to quality instruction. **When teachers are required to deal with misbehavior, the result is a loss of instruction time for other children. Parents should be involved in developing school plans and required to support and understand school discipline and management plans.** I received no training in discipline programs in college, although this may have changed since my college days. There are some excellent discipline programs available which may even help with consistency. Some excellent examples include Assertive Discipline, Positive Discipline, and Responsive School Discipline. There are many other effective programs available to both parents and schools.

Parent meetings to discuss school programming should be scheduled before school starts but are usually scheduled well into the school year. Classroom management expectations must be clearly understood by the parents before students enter school. The programs should emphasize the importance of safety for children in the school and minimize disruptions to the classroom.

Discipline management programs should praise positive behaviors, set clear expectations, and use calm consequences for both negative and positive behaviors. In their interactions teachers should make eye contact and get on the same level with children and teachers should carefully pick their battles. Effective teacher discipline programs should be practiced and emotion free. Most importantly, discipline programs should be school-wide for consistency.

Special education programs have created a myriad of terms to describe children who misbehave and may qualify for special assistance from the school. The federal government recognizes several labels that include emotional and behavioral disturbances. One common term is Oppositional Defiant Disorder (ODD). Children who are autistic sometimes also have an emotional disturbance. Children with Serious Emotional Disturbance (SED) may display inappropriate types of behavior or feelings under normal circumstances and children may also be saddled with the term Intermittent Explosive Disorder (IED) or simply Conduct Disorder (CD), a more serious label. Most of these children deal with impulse control, a situation more common with male students. This results in angry outbursts or aggression. One of the most common labels include attention deficit and hyperactivity disorder (ADHD). The last disorder to discuss is disruptive mood dysregulation disorder, a related disorder to some of the labels mentioned. Students assigned these labels should be entitled to special assistance. **If behavior is a common occurrence with your children, you can request an individual evaluation for your child and testing may be appropriate.**

Children with documented disabilities are entitled to instructional programs when they turn three years old. Make sure you contact the school if you feel your children need help. For example, a child with Trisomy 21, commonly known as Downs Syndrome, will qualify for services at age 3.

Recommended programs should include parents and become a vital part in the home environment. Consistency between the school and home is a key to deal with children with behavior issues.

RECOMMENDATION 10
Is Homework Valuable?

Homework can be helpful in the learning process. If the school does not require some homework, you should take the time to help your children at home. Read to your children often because this helps children develop a love for reading.

Many administrators, teachers, and parents have differing opinions about homework. **I believe some homework can be an effective learning experience. Most of the higher performing schools require homework.** I have seen some schools that assign almost too much homework, particularly in higher performing secondary schools. Spending two or three hours of homework a night may be too much for some students.

At the elementary level some homework can be valuable with certain conditions. It helps children to understand the value of learning and can get parents more involved in the instructional programs at school. Parents should create a good homework environment free of distractions for their children. If possible, it always helps for parents to work with their children. Make it a practice to read to your children or help them learn their math facts. The best elementary schools create recommendations for required homework. At the primary levels the amount of homework should never exceed more than 45 minutes and much less for the first few grades, unless the purpose of homework is to finish work not completed in class.

Your child's teacher should create consistent homework schedules. For example, Monday night should be reading night where a student reads a book for 15 minutes. Tuesday could be a math night where a student can practice solving problems or practice memorizing multiplication tables. Wednesdays might be a writing night or the next night to practice penmanship. Homework schedules can help get parents involved and they should always make sure their children consistently have quiet time for work at home. Parents should regularly interact with their children and, if necessary, help with their homework.

Most importantly, homework should not be required if teachers do not review work completed at home. Not doing so is wasting instruction time. If you are reading to your child there should be a process to help parents give feedback to the teacher. Be careful to choose topics of interest to children. My youngest grandson would love anything to do with baseball, so that would be a good starting point for him. I read to my two girls Grimms Fairy Tales or other classic literature. I chose the classic materials because of the challenging vocabulary. It became a memorable experience for me and my children.

RECOMMENDATION 11
Instruction Time Should Not Be Wasted

Make a serious effort to understand every school schedule, including breaks in classroom instruction for recess, lunches, teacher training, and special programs.

Children need sufficient time to learn and anything that has a negative effect on teaching time can be a real problem. This could be one of the worst problems in our elementary schools. Some children require more time to master skills. **The effectiveness of any elementary school program is also based on the quantity of time teachers have for instruction.** School personnel tend to work to improve the quality of teaching which is a good thing. However, the amount of time to teach is also extremely important. **Many elementary schools do not maximize valuable instruction time.** Either there are too many interruptions to the instructional schedule or worse, teaching time is taken away to provide for other activities.

Although there are many challenges in education today, think about the challenges were greater for American teachers around the end of the 19th and beginning of the 20th centuries. Often teachers in rural areas had to serve multiple grade levels in one-room schools. The effective use of teaching time was essential. The typical schedule of a one-room school serving four grades was incredible. The four different grade levels are noted by a letter. When the teacher was working with a particular group, the other level students quietly completed assignments or helped younger students or the students that needed extra help.

9:00		Opening Exercises	1:00		Roll Call, etc.
9:10	D	Reading and Spelling	1:05	D	Reading and Spelling
9:20	C	Primary Geography	1:15	C	Arithmetic

Time		Subject	Time		Subject
9:35	B	Primary Geography	1:30	B	Arithmetic
9:50	A	History or Geography	1:50	A	Arithmetic
10:10	D	Language Lessons	2:15		Writing and Drawing
10:25		Recess	2:35		Recess
10:40	C	Language Lessons	2:50	D	Object Lessons or Reading
10:55	B	Language Lessons	3:00	C	Reading and Spelling
11:25	A	Grammar	3:15	B	Reading and Spelling
11:50	D	Numbers	3:35	A	Reading and Spelling
12:00		Noon Recess	3:55		General Exercises
			4:00		Dismissal

Cooperative learning has been one of the important strategies used in many schools today. Just think how important it was in pioneer days. Now, if you were attentive to the above schedule, you would note that schools required a total of 6 hours of instruction or 360 minutes of instruction per day. Teachers were evaluated on their ability to adhere to schedules and the performance of their students. The quantity of instruction was an important element in education in rural America in those days!

Parents should focus on the amount of instruction time available at their school. The time educators teach is very important and that will be the subject of this recommendation. The quantity of instruction is critical in developing adequate student performance. In my view, excellent schools carefully cherish instruction time. **While the quality of instruction is very important, the amount of time teachers teach is not always as important to educators in school programming. It is a fact schools that value every minute of instruction time are going to be more effective in producing better student performance.** One of the best principals I knew kept a stopwatch and monitored release times, recess times, and dismissals. While many felt this was a little "over the top", the principal knew how important teaching time was in creating a good instructional program. The children in his school clearly outperformed all the other schools in his school district and school was among the best schools in his state.

There is a tremendous amount of wasted instruction time in some schools. Schools that maximize their use of instruction time are much more successful in producing better student achievement. Most states mandate minimal instruction time in statutory regulations. Unfortunately, little has been done to make sure even minimal daily instruction requirements are met. Other than calendar day requirements, little is done to monitor the actual teaching time taught.

Many school districts have early release days for teacher training that takes part of the instructional schedule and eliminates some of the time teachers need to work with students. **While it is true that teachers need continued professional growth through additional training, common in other professions, it should not be at the expense of student instruction time.** These schools are attempting to focus on quality teaching at the expense of the time they teach and that is wrong. I have noticed that the best schools have regular meetings with teachers to discuss instruction, but it is not time taken from the time teachers can teach. The teachers in the highest performing district in the area I live meet every morning to discuss and improve their programs before school starts.

The following recommendation will be especially hard for both students and parents to accept. **The best time for quality teaching time is the first few hours in the morning.** I have seen too many schools that schedule morning recesses, eliminating some of the best instruction time. If your children are enrolled in an elementary school that regularly schedules morning recesses, your children are losing quality teaching time. I volunteered to help at an elementary school in Texas years ago. School started at 8:15 am in the morning and I saw the first recess break at 9:15 am. That was just wrong!

To change this might be a difficult issue with your children. They enjoy recesses. I remember asking my youngest grandson telling me his favorite subject in school was recess. Here is where it gets tough because morning recesses also allow teachers a small break. **I realize that effective teaching is difficult, but the best schools avoid**

scheduling recesses during precious morning hours. Adequate time for lunch and recess provides a good break for all the students and teachers. I realize that "specials" such as music, physical education or library time can't always be scheduled in the afternoon and there are exceptions to my recommendations on morning instruction. My only point is schools should try their best to savor the morning time they have to teach.

I have observed hundreds of classes going to morning recess, normally for about 15 minutes. Getting the students lined up, to the playground, and back to the classroom almost always exceeds 15 minutes. **Just think about it. If the normal schoolyear is 180 days, saving just 15 minutes per day equals 9 or 10 school days per year (or in simple terms, almost two weeks of school). Now if you add additional afternoon breaks, the amount of wasted instruction could grow exponentially.** If the students have a nice lunch and recess break, there is really no reason for afternoon recesses unless they are an integral part of the school's physical education program.

If schools use an early release day during the school week, ask your principal what is done during training programs. Better yet, ask them if you can sit in on the training. Make sure you let your school administrators know that the quantity of time is important, especially if your children are struggling. **If one half day of teacher training is scheduled each week, your children have lost approximately twenty days of instruction during the school year.** That figure is huge and perhaps one of the most important negative factors that impact the time teachers work with children as well as student performance.

Even with recesses, I believe most honest teachers would admit they could improve their programs by saving 10 to 15 minutes of instruction per day. With morning and afternoon recesses, or teacher training time, you have given up nearly a month of instruction per school year.

I specifically remember contracting with a district to improve the performance of a failing school. The school had a school calendar with a two week vacation every quarter or nine weeks total. In addition, they had a summer vacation. While I was concerned with the quality of the teaching in the school and was charged with the responsibility of helping the school emerge from their failing status, I immediately became concerned about the amount of time lost in the schedule due to quarterly breaks. As a principal I was unable to change the district's calendar. The school had a two week break after nine weeks of school with a slightly shortened summer vacation. I addressed the issue with the teachers. **I discovered most of the better teachers were also concerned with the loss of instruction time and the skills children lose in those quarterly school breaks.** This was especially important for a school comprised of large numbers of non-English-speaking children who were struggling. I asked the teachers what they could do to address the scheduling issue. I was pleasantly surprised when a few of the teachers said they would be willing to volunteer to work a half day with the most struggling students during the break. **This confirmed my belief that most teachers really care about student performance. I can't tell you how much I appreciated the professionalism of those teachers.**

With a cadre of teacher volunteers who were not paid for the extra time, we identified the students who needed the most help. After doing so, we invited the parents of those children to a short parent meeting to discuss the problem in hopes we would get the parents to allow their children to attend school in the mornings of the quarterly breaks. Most of the children were English learners whose parents spoke only Spanish. A few of the students were also children identified as having a learning disability. Personal invitations were sent to the parents of those children noting we would provide refreshments and would be discussing the possibility of getting their children some extra help.

We provided general school testing information to the parents and then discussed the overall school's poor performance. The parents were able to see that their children needed help. We also provided

Spanish-speaking interpreters. Simple questions were answered such as will the children continue to have breakfast and lunch. Since the school was a Title 1 school (a school with a predominance of lower performing minority children), we were able to provide food service but unable to provide busing services. Our inability to provide transportation services did not affect the parents as most of those children lived close to school. All but one of the parents agreed to allow their children to participate. The one parent who chose not to allow their child to attend the school during the break was openly supportive but, due to personal issues, could not participate.

After one year of the extra help, the school's performance rating went from a failing rating to "performing plus", an unbelievable increase in student performance. While there were other factors that helped improve the students' performance, the amount of extra time to work with the children was a very positive element and a tribute to the professionalism of those teachers.

At the beginning of the year make sure you are aware of detailed school schedules. How many recess breaks are scheduled during the day and how long are the breaks? It will take more than a little encouragement from parents to help their children and teachers understand the importance of classroom instruction, especially if you are an advocate of eliminating morning recesses. **Support the school's effort to eliminate morning recesses because they are detrimental to the quantity of instruction**. Stand your ground and make sure the school administration understands your position! Influencing children to accept the fact that they will not have a morning recess can certainly be hard. Be strong and explain to your children that they don't need the break if they are to be successful in school.

There is also far too much time wasted with special events. This includes parent programs, parties, and fund-raising events to name a few. There is not a week where I read about children visiting a farm, having a "hat day", planting trees, or making field trips that eliminate a portion of instructional time. Perhaps the most ridiculous field trip experience I remember happened in Oregon where a student told me he had visited milk dairies four times during his first five years of school. I am not opposed to field trips if they augment the instructional program. Parents and children really enjoy parent programs and I support such efforts. **Field trips should be aligned with instructional programs. The practices for special school programs should be scheduled after school or during music instruction time. Special programs are important, but participation should not include the use of school instruction time.**

Sometimes classrooms or all grade levels plan a special program for the parents. This may be one of the most difficult recommendations in this book. I am not a proponent of eliminating events that children and parents enjoy. But that time should not be taken from instruction time. I remember one school wasting the better part of several days preparing for a school carnival sponsored by parents for money raising purposes. They raised a huge amount of money and that was great, but not as important as wasting instruction time.

Although I have a college minor in the humanities and taught art history at the community college level, **art projects at the primary levels (grades kindergarten through third) can also be time wasters in elementary school.** I have personally seen so many situations where a writing assignment is made, but the children spend much more time drawing pictures to accompany their story than writing. Don't get me wrong, it is important. I am not against art but believe it can become a waste of valuable teaching time if implemented improperly.

I once hired a wonderful art education specialist to evaluate this issue in an elementary school where I was a principal. She came back and told me the methods used in the school were not good and that we needed to revamp our art program. She told me the primary teachers are using the art portion of their classes to take a break from teaching. She was happy to help teachers understand what is important and how to use proven art concepts for the younger children. Art is important and teachers need to understand how to use that media to help children learn.

I will never forget one teacher that told me "The whole week before Christmas break and the last week of school were a total waste and good instruction was simply not possible because the students were too excited." That was one of the most idiotic statements I have ever heard as a former principal. **Children will perform to imposed expectations** and I can assure you the instruction of that teacher was poor for that week. Her students consistently performed poorly on the state mandated testing program.

Full Day Kindergarten Programs

Parents with incoming kindergarten children should take advantage of schools that offer full-day kindergarten programs. Believe me when I say that children enrolled in schools that offer all-day programs give children a tremendous start in learning. As an administrator, I was responsible for creating the first full-day kindergarten program in one of the first districts where I worked. At that time all the many other elementary schools in the area offered only half-day programs. Our district received several anonymous complaints that we were guilty of child abuse of those kindergarten children. As with the case for all grades, our children performed better than all the other elementary schools in the entire area. Most importantly, the children enjoyed learning! **Full-day programs have now become more common, so make sure your new kindergarten student gets a better start!**

RECOMMENDATION 12
Competency Testing

The current trend in America is to lower standards in the name of equity. Support efforts to make sure your children are academically ready for advancement to the next grade.

Higher standards have been diluted over the years. For example, some testing requirements for admission to college have been eliminated. The lack of competencies and the dilution of admission standards in colleges may be the ultimate reason why demonstrated competencies are important in our elementary schools.

It is important for parents to support strengthening standards beginning with elementary schools. **All students should demonstrate competency in the English language by third grade and those children having difficulty should continue to participate in special English language or other programs until a workable level of proficiency is attained. All eighth graders should demonstrate proficiency in English, writing, history, mathematics, and the Constitution before they leave a middle school or junior high school.** There are far too many students placed in what has been termed transitional programs in high school due to the lack of proficiency in one of the basic subjects.

Unlike many European nations that require students to demonstrate performance as they advance in their studies, the idea of competency testing is beginning to get sparse support in American schools. **Parents, support competency testing in elementary schools and clearly communicate to your children the fact they need to perform at acceptable levels as they move through the educational system.** Social promotion is common in our schools and is a disservice to your children.

Competency testing should not hurt equity efforts to help all students achieve acceptable levels of success. Equity should not result in the downgrading of standards. If we are to achieve excellence in education, this subject should be at the top of a debate. In my view, the efforts to achieve equity means we should create effective programs to deal with the special needs of all children. **Every child should be the focus of efforts to develop competencies. Many children deal with unfortunate situations and teachers need to ensure all students have a chance to succeed. Push for special programs needed to help all students perform at acceptable levels.**

To achieve this goal may require we move students through the system as they demonstrate competencies.

    a. Students should have a decent command of the English language and read with competency before moving from elementary school.

    b. Students should demonstrate a reasonable command of mathematics before moving from elementary school.

    c. Students should be able to write legibly and with some creativity before moving from elementary school.

    d. Students should demonstrate a basic knowledge of the American constitution before moving from elementary levels.

    e. Students should be able to demonstrate a basic knowledge of American history before moving from elementary school.

    f. Students should be able to demonstrate a decent command of basic geographic concepts before moving from elementary schools.

    g. Students should be able to pass most of the physical skills considered important in the President's Physical Fitness program. Far too many of our young children are obese and that is an issue that should be addressed by both schools and parents.

My grandson is enrolled in a college graduate program in neuroscience in Europe. He must pass and demonstrate competencies before a committee of instructors before he is awarded his master's degree. **Competency testing is an important part of education in many European countries, and I think it could provide the motivation for students to work harder in American schools. With assistance, minority children with special needs, especially in language, can succeed and achieve higher levels of competencies.** Although I was a decent student in elementary school, I always had a small amount of doubt that my final report card would recommend advancement to the next grade. That doubt created some motivation for me.

Good News!

A bright spot in the competency issue is the establishment of more technical and vocational programs. These programs provide training that can help older students exiting public education become contributing members of society. For example, the State of Arizona has created Technical Education Districts in most counties. This provides the opportunity for students to participate in more vocational programs while attending school. I know of several middle school students who have also taken basic college courses for free credit before entering high school. I know of high school students that graduate with an entire year or two of college liberal arts courses completed. Not all students need to attend college and would be much more productive if they received more technical education in addition to a basic instructional program.

I remember a middle school student in middle student who did absolutely nothing in class. He was not any kind of disciplinary problem but just didn't care about his studies. I had many long conversations with the student to determine what he wanted to do in life. He told me he is only in school because it was required, but that his only work goal was to do auto body work. He told me he would inherit his father's auto body repair business and that he is already proficient in many of the skills required to function at very high levels. He also told me he enjoyed working on cars more than anything. Having been a car collector for many years,

I better understood his issue. A good body worker can make very good money. I appealed to him to understand the importance of basic math as applied to the business and he tried a little more but was never going to be a good student academically. If his dream of becoming a good auto body repair person comes true, he will be successful in life and make a good living,

RECOMMENDATION 13
The Importance of Effective Teacher Training Institutions

Make sure your child's teachers are properly certified. In view of the changes in the demographics in America's schools and the shortage of teachers, it is important to make sure you are familiar with the qualifications of the teachers that work with your children.

Most parents realize that effective teachers are the most important component of student learning. **The quality of the instructional methods used by individual teachers will impact the performance of the students. The quality of teacher training programs can vary widely throughout the United States.**

Parents can usually access certification information of teachers in their school by accessing the appropriate website. To be fair, certification requirements have increased in recent years to better accommodate more students, particularly non-English-speaking children. It is common to see schools hiring teachers with emergency certificates who are in the process of completing all new certification requirements. This does not mean they are poor teachers. However, it is good information in the process of choosing a school. In addition, there is a documented shortage of teachers in our country. That is an issue that has had a negative effect on the quality of the programs offered at the elementary level.

The education of new teachers needs to improve. They need to be taught using proven effective methods and programs. College instructors need to focus on teaching proven research strategies. Further, they need to provide accurate and unbiased information and not indoctrinate their students with only one philosophical position. College professors should concentrate on monitoring their students beyond the four years their students spend in college. They should be willing to give assistance to new graduates that might be struggling.

When I was a student teacher, I was visited only one time and I paid expenses for the single visit by my advisor. He interviewed my master teacher for fifteen minutes and that was it. I received a high rating and was lucky to have had a great master teacher with which to work. **The best schools have master teachers whose main duties are to work with teachers and students in the classroom on a continual basis.**

Teacher colleges should be required to monitor the effectiveness of their graduates more thoroughly. This could be done by tracking their students and examining the performance of their former students in creating the best student outcomes. Testing information is publicly accessible and should be a major asset of teacher training institutions. When looking at colleges, potential students should carefully examine what courses are taught in their programs. Courses should be more practical and less philosophical. Invite successful former students to provide information to undergraduate students on the challenges they face as new teachers. Most importantly, colleges should invite the most successful principals to talk to their students about their successes, focusing on the methods to create the best student performance.

RECOMMENDATION 14
The Demographic Makeup of American Schools

How many students are enrolled in your school that are non-English-speaking students? In many schools, teachers are dealing with large numbers of children who lack an understanding of the English language, a situation that may have a negative influence on the time teachers are able to spend with students who already have a solid grasp of the language.

America has been saturated with large numbers of foreign students who have been allowed to illegally enter our country in the past several years. Some estimates put the number of illegal entrants at more than seven million. Although most seem to be military aged males, there have also been many school age children. American public schools can't prevent non-English-speaking illegal migrant children from receiving a free and appropriate public education, although the cost of this education is not free to the American taxpayers.

School districts must only establish the fact that these students are residents of the district and are not allowed to act as immigration officials. Can you imagine the pressure this puts on our teachers? **Large numbers of non-English speaking children force teachers to spend tremendous amounts of time trying to help students overcome language deficits.** This forces teachers to concentrate on students who are performing at lower levels, perhaps at the expense of students who are capable of learning at much higher levels.

It is estimated that at least ten percent of elementary school children are English language learners, although many border cities and districts have almost all students who are learning English. More importantly, it is critical parents understand that schools are dealing with students from well over a hundred and fifty different nations.

That makes a difficult language situation worse. I think I understand the movement for equity in our country. But is it equitable for the needs of students capable of learning at higher levels not addressed because our teachers are spending more time teaching some students basic English? **In short, public schools are forced to concentrate more time dealing with lower performing students because of language deficiencies than addressing the needs students who are ready to move to higher levels of learning.**

Check to see how many children are learning English in school. This information might be helpful in choosing an elementary school. If the numbers are significant, you need to get information from the school regarding how the situation affects dominant English speakers. There are some excellent schools that have only non-English-speaking children. However, this may affect the quality of programs for children who are capable of learning at higher levels even though many non-English speaking children may possess higher abilities. Some parents may wish their children to have the opportunity to experience second languages and cultures. In this case, the language issues may be less important and a positive situation for those parents and their children.

RECOMMENDATION 15

Programs Such as the 1619 Project and Social and Emotional Learning

Avoid schools that have become progressive training grounds, teaching only one side of an issue. Many of the contemporary issues for which schools are dealing should be the responsibility of parents.

Some of America's schools have become philosophical progressive training grounds. **I could devote an entire book on programs that promote very liberal progressive ideas that address only one side of issues.** Critical race theory and social and emotional learning are programs that give students only one look at issues. I am a firm believer in educating students about issues in our world, but to do so from only one perspective is not right. It is important to realize that teachers should present facts and avoid their opinions. Teachers should accept the fact that children can be critical thinkers, something all teachers need to understand. Far too often teachers will, either purposely or not, present their opinions of important issues which will influence the beliefs of the children.

Recently, the State of Arizona approved the use of PragerU materials for use in the State's schools. The issue can be summed up in one simple opening statement on the PragerU website. "Sadly, many American schools are replacing education with indoctrination. Instead of learning how to think critically and develop reading and writing skills, our children are being taught radical ideas about systemic racism, gender fluidity, and anti-American ideas without their consent." Care should be taken to make sure we present facts and that all issues are dealt with fairly. This includes the conservative philosophies of PragerU. Elementary teachers should concentrate only on teaching the most important basic skills.

That brings me to the recent controversy of establishing common core standards. Unless I am wrong, many parents are opposed to the idea of a common core curriculum because parents believe in local control in each community. That is, each community should be able to establish their own standards for education. Additionally, other parents fear some standards are too advanced for young learners. In my opinion, there are very important basic skills that all children should master, but it would be unprofessional to not provide advanced skills for some students.

I believe we should have one national test that covers the most important basic skills that would be administered to all the country's children. Doing so would allow parents to better understand where their children stand in comparison to other students in the country. This is especially important with the most important basic skills. This also gives schools and teachers a clear understanding of the average levels of learning from state to state.

However, it is important to also establish higher standards and skills that all children can strive to learn. Encourage your children to achieve and master required skills. Encourage the children to meet the highest of standards. Your help is so important, especially in the elementary grades. Taking an active role in the education of your children and communicate the fact you support efforts to do well in school. Carefully review grade reports and help children understand you expect their best effort in school.

In elementary school my own children knew that I expected them to perform and do well in school. Early in their education, I gave them a silver dollar for every A grade received. I know this was controversial and I received my share of negative comments about this practice. As the children got older, they knew it was important to achieve and they eventually understood it was important to get good grades without tangible rewards. I was able to back off because they knew it was academically important and wanted to do well in school. They did achieve at very high levels in public school and college. Although we were only a family of four, my family has accumulated a total of ten college degrees. Most importantly, they continue to achieve at very high levels in the work environment.

Parents have the right to know what is taught and likely most parents want their children to be exposed to both sides of important issues. Give children accurate facts and encourage them to understand the clear facts in all issues.

Is there anyone who can justify to me the value of bringing drag queens into schools to perform for our young children? Children are easily influenced and bringing drag queens into schools is just wrong! **Avoid any school or district that has a history of promoting only progressive ideas and programs to our children.**

RECOMMENDATION 16
Technology in Education

Understand the appropriate role technology plays in education.

Schools are heavily into technology which, if used properly, can be an effective learning tool. Computers and computer tablets can be very helpful learning tools.

However, I have seen many primary school children in grades one through three wasting too much time typing with one finger when they could be printing or writing words. The use of computers and technology can provide a wealth of information for our children. However, computers should not replace the role of the teacher, especially in the primary grades.

Computers can be used in testing and evaluation and sometimes even important instruction. **Computer tablets should not replace the emphasis on penmanship and writing.** Problems with tablets and the time it takes children to type words is wasting direct teacher instruction time. Children are excited about tablets and computers, but I have seen too much wasted time, especially in the first few grades. As children advance in grades and become more capable readers, the use of computers, particularly in reading stories and checking for comprehension or practicing math problems, is valuable.

I am particularly impressed with interactive teaching boards, sometimes referred to as smart boards. Interactive teaching boards are large computers and can be used effectively with all levels in elementary schools. They can be especially useful in critical instructional areas, including phonics, penmanship, and writing skills. Students can access many excellent computer applications. For example, Google

Earth would allow the teacher to visually access physical phenomena anywhere in the world. They would be very helpful in a history or geography lesson. A teacher can help students learn note taking or improve their writing skills.

If I were a new teacher, I would buy an interactive teaching board with my own money. Their potential as a learning tool is phenomenal. But the cost of technology is often so high that it is impossible for some schools to purchase equipment. This is especially true due to the increases in maintenance and operations costs, the majority of which includes teacher salaries.

It is my recommendation that parents carefully look at how they use cell phones and computer tablets with young children. Dependence on games early can create issues later in education because you are only creating visual learners. It is distressing to me to see toddlers being entertained with cell phones and computer tablets. Be selective in what applications you allow your children to use if you need some strategy to entertain your children. Parents should limit the use computers, tablets, and cell phones to instructional applications that include instructional games children like. I am especially proud of my children who chose not to allow cell phone use for their children until the age of 13 and then limited use to some selective texting and phone use, restricting the use of their phones for other social media. They continually monitor their children's cell phone use until their children reach the age of 18. Many schools are beginning to restrict the use of cell phones which I think is a very wise decision. Parents should be very concerned with their children's use of social media applications.

Technological advances provide valuable tools that will help our teachers, but we can't forget the importance of the basic concepts that once made American education the best in the world.

RECOMMENDATION 17
Charter Schools vs Public Schools

Charter schools may provide an appropriate alternative to public schools and sometimes offer more emphasis on basic education. Charter schools are presently producing slightly higher student performance than public schools.

The charter school movement has grown each year. Currently there are forty-five states that offer charter school programs. Almost four million students are enrolled in charter schools in America. Originally the concept of the charter school movement was to close the gap between students of color and white students. That seems to be one of the successful components of charters as their minority students generally out-perform minority public school students.

Charter schools are publicly funded and tuition free. They are usually different from public schools because they are allowed more flexibility in approaches to curriculum and instruction. They often offer different philosophical options and models in comparison to public schools. The options are particularly important for parents who desire a choice, particularly if they are not able financially to afford tuition to parochial schools. In short, charter schools have more flexibility than public schools. According to national figures, charter school students perform slightly better than public school students. Some charter schools and even some excellent public schools are so popular they use lottery systems to determine which new students are enrolled.

Parents should perform due diligence in deciding what schools are best for their children. Look at curriculum and instructional programs used at both public and charter schools. I can assure you that there are some excellent charter and public schools. The degree of parental success is dependent on the issues previously discussed in "Fixing American Elementary Schools: A Parent's Guide."

RECOMMENDATION 18

Review Information on State Rankings, Paying Close Attention to the Programs of the Best Schools

How does your state compare to others in student performance and other factors?

The latest U.S. News and World Report rates the performance of each state using a variety of K-12 indicators. The most important indicator is student performance and an understanding of academic subject matter. The results from the National Assessment of Educational Progress also measures other subject areas, including the arts, civics, geography, mathematics, reading, science, U.S. history, writing, economics, and technology. There are many other factors that should be considered in the evaluation of the quality of education in each state. The following list is the most recent state rankings for your information.

1. Florida
2. New Jersey
3. Massachusetts
4. Colorado
5. Utah
6. Wisconsin
7. Nebraska
8. Connecticut
9. New York
10. Washington
11. Virginia
12. Illinois
13. Iowa
14. Wyoming
15. Vermont

16. North Carolina
17. Indiana
18. South Dakota
19. New Hampshire
20. California
21. Minnesota
22. Idaho
23. Maryland
24. Hawaii
25. Montana
26. Kansas
27. Georgia
28. North Dakota
29. Ohio
30. Delaware
31. Missouri
32. Kentucky
33. Tennessee
34. Maine
35. Texas
36. Pennsylvania
37. Michigan
38. Nevada
39. Oregon
40. Rhode Island
41. Mississippi
42. South Carolina
43. Arkansas
44. Alabama
45. Arizona
46. Louisiana
47. West Virginia
48. Oklahoma
49. Alaska
50. New Mexico

The following list includes a few of the best elementary schools in each state. The problem with the limited list provided is that it does not include many of the other great schools that have excellent student performance. The schools listed were selected because they consistently create excellent student performance and have been rated very high in each state. Some of these best schools are charter schools, magnets schools, and public schools. It was difficult to get specific information about reading instruction in the schools. However, I do know most of the following schools use intensive phonics instruction in their beginning reading programs. Some of the following schools use common core standards which include phonics.

This list is provided to help parents understand the performance of the best schools. This is not a recommendation to enroll your student in the schools. I suggest you look at what these schools are doing to create such incredible student performance and ratings. Then you can find a school closer to your location that is a closer to some of the nation's best schools.

Alabama
Eicholdmertz School of Math and Science
Crestline Elementary School
Mt. Laurel Elementary School

Alaska
Huffman Elementary
Eagle Academy Charter School
Northern Lights ABC K-8 School

Arizona
BASIS Schools
Chandler Traditional Academy
Knox Gifted Academy
Challenger Basic School
Weinberg Gifted Academy

Arkansas
Haas Hall Academy
Baker Interdistrict Elementary School
Willowbrook Elementary School

California (When searching the state's website, the internet yielded mostly private schools.)
William Faria Elementary School
North Star Academy
The Nueva School (A private school with tuition exceeding $50,000 per year)

Colorado
Peak to Peak Charter School
Challenge School
Polaris Elementary School

Connecticut
West School of New Canaan
Sherman School
Stamford Charter School for Excellence

Delaware
Newark Charter School
Lake Forest North Elementary School
Allen Frear Elementary School

Florida
Jacksonville Beach Elementary School
Pine View School
Somerset Academy Miramar South

Georgia
Kittredge Magnet School
Britt David Elementary Computer Magnet Academy
Daves Creek Elementary School

Hawaii

Momilani Elementary School
Hokulani Elementary School
Myron B. Thompson Academy

Idaho

North Idaho Stem Charter Academy
Highlands Elementary School
Discovery Elementary School

Illinois

Skinner North Elementary School
Brook Forest Elementary School
Oak Elementary School

Indiana

Eagle Elementary School
Paramount Brookside
Seven Oaks Classical School

Iowa

West Bend-Mallard Elementary School
Hopewell Elementary
Pleasant View Elementary School

Kansas

Corinth Elementary School
Prairie Creek Elementary School
Bradley Elementary School

Kentucky

Sublimity Elementary School
Carter City Elementary School
Anchorage Independent School

Louisiana
A.E. Phillips Laboratory School
The Willow School New Orleans
Belle Chasse Academy

Maine
Yarmouth Elementary School
Friendship Village School
Harrington Elementary School

Maryland
Close Spring Elementary
Westbrook Elementary
Travilah Elementary

Massachusetts
Field Elementary School
Woodland Elementary School
John D. Hardy Elementary School

Michigan
Gallimore Elementary School
Webster Elementary School
Crestwood Accelerated Program

Minnesota
Atheneum Elementary
Gate 4/5
St. Croix Preparatory Academy Lower

Mississippi
Laurel Magnet School of the Arts
Bayou View Elementary School
Barack H. Obama Elementary School

Missouri
Mound City Elementary School
Mallinckrodt A.B.I. Elementary School
Richland Elementary

Montana
Morning Star School
Jefferson School
Longfellow School

Nebraska
Hitchcock Elementary School
Blue Sage Elementary School
Aldridge Elementary

Nevada
Ted Hunsberger Elementary
Roy Gomm Elementary
Pinecrest Academy of Nevada Inspirada

New Hampshire
Rye Elementary School
Bernice A. Ray School
Lafayette Regional School

New Jersey
Lincoln-Hubbard Elementary School
Glenwood School
Princeton Charter School

New Mexico
Mountain Elementary
Hubert H. Humphrey Elementary
Double Eagle Elementary

New York
PS 77 Lower Lab School
New Explorations Into Science Tech and Math School
The Academy for Excellence Through the Arts

North Carolina
Lincoln Academy
Metrolina Reg Scholars Academy
Rea View Elementary

North Dakota
Longfellow Elementary School
Larimore Elementary School
Mis-Mohall Elementary School

Ohio
Hilltop Elementary School
Parkside Elementary School
Miller City Elementary School

Oklahoma
Clegern Elementary School
Oakdale Public School
Chisholm Elementary School

Oregon
Findley Elementary
Jacob Wismer Elementary School
Westridge Elementary School

Pennsylvania
Bower Hill Elementary School
Fairview Elementary School
Bradford Woods Elementary School

Rhode Island
Community School
Nayatt School
Fort Barton School

South Carolina
Buist Academy
Augusta Circle Elementary
Belton Preparatory Academy

South Dakota
Challenge Center – 51
Valley Springs Elementary – 04
Warner Elementary – 02

Tennessee
Mcfadden School of Excellence
Merrol Hyde Magnet School
Discovery School

Texas
William B, Travis Vanguard for the Academically Talented and Gifted
Martha & Josh Morris Math and Engineering Elementary
Overton Park Elementary

Utah
Sunrise School
Peruvian Park School
Cottonwood School

Vermont
Marion W. Cross School
Barnard Academy
Hinesburg Elementary School

Virginia
Kingston Elementary
Old Donation School
Poplar Tree Elementary

Washington
Cascadia Elementary
Challenge Elementary
Decatur Elementary School

West Virginia
Greenmont Elementary School
Evans Elementary School
Holtz Elementary School

Wisconsin
Mill Valley Elementary
Kohler Elementary
Wauwatosa Stem

Wyoming
Poder Academy
Sagebrush Elementary
Wilson Elementary

Note: Kentucky, Montana, Nebraska, North Dakota, Vermont, and West Virginia do not have charter schools. The statistics of the above schools are influenced by ethnic status and other factors such as annual income of parents. The location of the school is certainly a factor in classifying schools. The U.S. News and World Report is an excellent source of information.

CONCLUSION

I hope that this book helps you understand how you can get the best possible elementary education for your children.

Although there are some wonderful public and charter schools in America, it takes parental involvement to improve our educational system. Make sure you at least consider the recommendations provided. Many states are legislating changes in the way we teach reading to include phonics instruction. I believe that American public schools have recently been given an important message and that the current situation will eventually change for the better. I am pleased that state legislators are beginning to understand that we have abandoned much of what works. I think education in America is at least moving in the right direction!

I have one last thought that everyone needs to understand. **Change is not easy and getting educators to understand what is needed to improve education is difficult**. In fact, making positive changes as an educator in schools may even put your job at risk, which makes the role of parents even more important. As an administrator I often had to fight hard to get things done and that almost always caused me a measure of grief. Something as simple as getting elementary teachers to understand the importance of phonics in reading programs was an incredible challenge.

I had many honest and open discussions with my teachers. It was difficult to get them to understand that their main objective was to focus on what works in the classroom, particularly in making sure they used phonics instruction in reading programs. Teachers should always work to improve student performance. It is important that all educational leaders accept their responsibility to improve learning as measured by improved student performance.

Teachers, especially when grouped together, render a lot of political power, particularly with school board members. I recommend parents take a more active role in establishing good communications with school board members and teachers. Let them know your concerns and make sure they represent the values of your community.

Be active in making sure the makeup of your school board represents the philosophy of the community. School board members should make every decision based on the needs of the children they serve. They should always ask themselves how will my next decision effect the students I serve? How will my decision improve the educational system for our children?

At the end of the year school board members should formally evaluate the progress their school district makes in improving student performance. They should carefully examine what has been done to improve their program.

School board members should establish goals and measurable objectives at the beginning of each school year. It is important the school board members understand the difference between a general goal and a measurable objective. For example, a goal might be to show improvement in the performance of the children they serve on required testing programs. Perhaps it may even be appropriate to allow the administrators and teachers to establish the objectives to meet those goals. But it is critical to hold everyone responsible for achieving the goals they establish.

District goals should always include student performance as measured by annual testing performance outcomes. During the school year they should check progress in meeting the measurable goals and objectives. After mandated testing results for the schools are available, they should carefully evaluate progress, something often sadly lacking in many school districts. School board members should expect progress and there is nothing more important than an annual review of progress. It is also important to add progress in meeting goals into salary negotiations. What progress has been made and how effectively did we address our annual goals?

One of my college professors accused me of being "out of touch" because I was too much into "back to the basics". His point was that all schools teach the basics, something for which I don't totally agree. My professor didn't understand or accept the fact that the changes I hoped to make were supported by extensive educational research. Sadly, he passed before I could show him the tremendous progress made in student performance in my schools. No teacher or principal should ever give up on trying to improve education in America.

Effective schools create a clear mission and make sure the staff supports that mission. Every child should be given the opportunity to learn because enough time is allotted to teaching basic skills with a minimum of disruptions. We should establish high expectations and frequently monitor student progress.

Positive changes require teamwork, and that team must include parents. Don't forget that parental involvement is the most important factor in helping schools improve. Get involved with your child's school because it is one of the best things you can do to make sure your children are successful in life.

Now you know what is important and, if needed, you can fix the elementary education for your children!